Thomas Chippendale
1718–1779

A Celebration of
British Craftsmanship
and Design

The Chippendale Society

2018

THIS BOOKLET ACCOMPANIES THE EXHIBITION HELD
AT LEEDS CITY MUSEUM, 9 FEBRUARY–9 JUNE 2018

Published by The Chippendale Society

ISBN: 978 1 9999229 0 0

Text © 2018 the authors

Illustrations © 2018 as credited in captions. All Harewood House images reproduced by courtesy of
the Harewood House Trust

FRONT COVER: Armchair, *c.* 1774, from the Tapestry Room, Newby Hall. Mr and Mrs
Richard Compton

BACK COVER: Statue of Thomas Chippendale, carved by Albert Hodge, 1905. West
façade of the Victoria and Albert Museum, London

Designed and produced in the UK by Derek Brown and Jackie Maidment

CHIPPENDALE
300
1718
2018

FOREWORD

Thomas Chippendale is still without doubt most famous furniture maker and designer of Georgian Britain. For at least 150 years his name has been synonymous with beautifully made furniture in a restrained (or sometimes not-so-restrained) Rococo style, and very obviously British. The fact that some of his finest work, and that of his workshop, belongs to the later neo-Classical period has also long been recognised and has only served to add to his reputation.

It seems appropriate that a major exhibition should be held in Leeds in 2018, the tercentenary of Chippendale's birth in Otley, just twelve miles north-west of the city. The Chippendale Society, founded in 1965 to promote appreciation of the work of Thomas Chippendale Senior and Junior, has taken the lead in co-ordinating a nation-wide celebration of his work and legacy with a group of historic houses and organisations collectively known as Chippendale 300. Each of the participating members is arranging its own programme of events to bring the achievements of 'the Shakespeare of British furniture' to a wider public.

The exhibition *Thomas Chippendale: a celebration of British craftsmanship and design 1718–79* is the first of these events and is intended to be a flagship for the rest of the project. It is a partnership between Leeds Museums and Galleries and the Chippendale Society: the former providing the exhibition organisation, and the latter most of the funding and the curatorial expertise. The Society is greatly indebted to John Roles, Head of Service, and his dedicated team for their hard work and forbearance during the long period of preparation, particularly Ruth Martin, Exhibitions Curator, Jen Kaines, Collections Manager, and Christine Bradley, Project Registrar. Leeds Museums and Galleries are supported by Leeds City Council and Arts Council England.

There have been several exhibitions devoted to Chippendale: since 1951 they have almost all been held at Leeds and it is instructive to see how their approach has changed. We hope that this exhibition, being held in a neutral space at the Museum in which the objects can be appreciated as individual works of art on their own terms and in interesting juxtapositions, will enable visitors to enjoy some of the finest English furniture of the eighteenth century. We have tried not to be dogmatic: not everything in the exhibition is by Chippendale, or even from his workshop. Even so, they all have a story to tell of their relationship to the great man. By bringing the tale up to the present day we have suggested how his legacy has permeated into our collective national consciousness.

This publication, together with the full catalogue to be published in April 2018 in which all the exhibits will be discussed in detail, has been generously supported by Ronald Phillips, John Morton Morris, the Nicholas and Judith Goodison Charitable Trust, the Furniture

History Society, Mr and Mrs Patrick Walker, Mr and Mrs David Kirkby, Lisa White and Mr Thomas Lange, to whom we are very grateful.

The principal sponsor of the exhibition is The Monument Trust which has been a long-term supporter of the Chippendale Society. We have also been generously supported by the Leeds Art Fund (Christopher Gilbert Fund), Ronald Phillips, Tomasso Brothers Fine Art, Last Cawthra Feather, Godson and Coles Ltd, Apter Fredericks Ltd, the Leeds Philosophical and Literary Society, Charles Lumb & Son, the Verdon Smith Charitable Trust, Lisa White, Butchoff Antiques, Arthur Brett, Thomas Coulborn and Sons, the Friends of Leeds Museums, the Friends of the Historic Houses Association, de Gournay and by others who wish to remain anonymous. We have been greatly encouraged by their enthusiasm and help.

We are indebted to the lenders to the exhibition and their staff who have facilitated our requests for loans, led by Her Majesty The Queen and the Royal Collections Trust; the Prince of Wales and the Great Steward of Scotland's Dumfries House Trust (Charlotte Rostek); the Earl and Countess of Harewood and the staff of the Harewood House Trust (Ann Sumner, Marie-Astrid Martin, Rebecca Burton); Lord Ronaldshay; Lord St Oswald (President of the Chippendale Society); Mr and Mrs Richard Compton; Michael Lipitch; the Trustees of the Victoria and Albert Museum (Leela Meinertas); the National Museums on Merseyside at the Lady Lever Art Gallery (Alyson Pollard); the National Trust at Nostell Priory (Christopher Rowell, Sarah Shaw and Simon McCormack); the Trustees of the Firle Settled Estates and Deborah Gage; the Paxton House Trust (Fiona Salvesen Murrell and David Jones); the Burton Constable Foundation (Kelly Wainwright) ; the York Civic Trust at Fairfax House (Hannah Phillips); Leeds Museums and Galleries (Ian Fraser, Rachel Conroy and Adam Toole). Others who have given us invaluable help include David Beevers, Rufus Bird, James Caverhill, Althea and Henrietta Dundas Bekker, Stuart Gill, John Hardy, Morrison Heckscher, Houghtons of York (Carvers), David Jones, Sarah Medlam, Hugh Wedderburn (Master Carver's Association), Lisa White and the Hon Cara Willoughby. Dame Rosalind Savill and Anthony Wells-cole have kindly provided additional text in their own fields of expertise for the main catalogue. Norman Taylor has been our principal photographer and has produced some magnificent images enabling us to see Chippendale's work in its full glory. Finally, we are grateful for the hard work, support and enthusiasm of the Chippendale Society Committee, without whom neither the exhibition nor the Society could exist.

Every student of Chippendale's work is conscious of the extraordinary debt owed to the late Christopher Gilbert (1936–1998), late Keeper of Temple Newsam House and Director of Leeds Art Galleries, whose magisterial *Life and Work of Thomas Chippendale* (1978) is a continuing source of information and reference. Finally, Judith Goodison's magnificent study of Thomas Chippendale Junior appeared just as we were going to press.

ADAM BOWETT, MELISSA GALLIMORE AND JAMES LOMAX

THOMAS CHIPPENDALE'S LIFE AND CAREER

Thomas Chippendale was born in Otley, near Leeds, and baptised in All Saints Church on 5 June 1718 (1). He was the only son of John Chippendale and Mary Drake, who married in July 1715. John Chippendale was a carpenter and joiner, as were other members of his extended family in and around Wharfedale. His house is thought to have been on the site now occupied by the Skipton Building Society in Boroughgate. After Mary's death in 1729 John remarried and had six more children, whose descendants continued to live in Otley.

It is not known where Thomas was trained, but it is thought that, having received some initial tuition either with his father or with a relative, he went to York to work as a cabinet-maker. This was probably with Richard Wood (fl. 1726–72), who ordered eight copies of the *Director* when it was first published in 1754.

Thomas retained his links with York and Yorkshire throughout his life, both through fellow tradesmen in York and Wakefield, and through the wealthy patrons whose houses he furnished. There is a longstanding tradition that some of his early career was spent working at Nostell Priory, near Wakefield, perhaps under the tutelage of the architect James Paine, but no evidence has yet been found to support it.

Nothing further is known about Chippendale's life or work until, at the age of twenty-nine, he married Catherine Redshaw in St George's Chapel, Mayfair, on 19 May 1748. Their first child, Thomas Jnr, was born in April 1749, and between Christmas 1749 and summer 1752 the Chippendale family lived in Conduit Court, off Long Acre. From there they moved to Northumberland Court off the Strand (2) before finally settling in St Martin's Lane in December 1753. Each move marked an increase in prosperity, indicated by the increase of the properties' rateable value from £12 to £22 to £124 (3 & 4).

The few years between his marriage and establishing himself in St Martin's Lane were pivotal for Chippendale. He had developed a strong working relationship with the designer and engraver Matthias Darly and, either through Darly or some other tutor, had mastered drawing in the Rococo style with which his name is forever associated. He also conceived his plan to create the most comprehensive furniture design book yet published in England but, lacking the capital for such an ambitious venture, he formed a partnership with

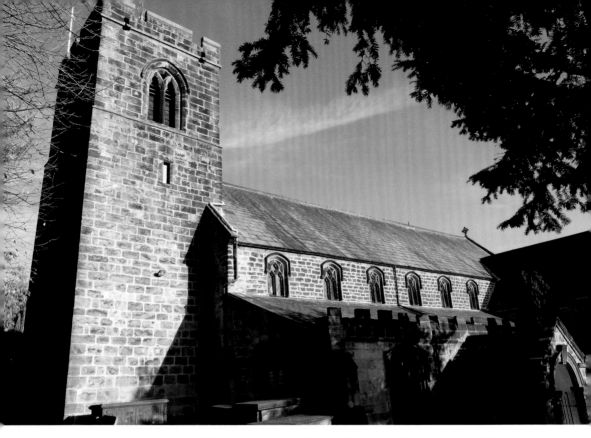

1 All Saints' Church, Otley, where Chippendale was baptised on 5 June 1718.
Lawrence Ross

James Rannie, a Scottish businessman and entrepreneur. It was probably Rannie who provided the funds both to set up the business in St Martin's Lane and to publish *The Gentleman and Cabinet-Maker's Director* in 1754 (**5**)

Chippendale claimed that he had been encouraged to publish by 'persons of distinction but of eminent taste', suggesting a hinterland of fashionable existing customers including the Earl of Burlington. As its title made clear, the book was aimed at both the buyers and the makers of fine furniture, 'to guide the one in the choice and the other in the execution of the designs'. It was in effect a manifesto of contemporary Rococo taste, demonstrating the infinite variations which could be achieved by a skilled craftsman working in the Gothic, Chinese or Modern styles. Advertisements appeared in the press inviting pre-publication subscriptions for a large folio with 160 plates at £1-10s in sheets or £1-14s bound, limited to 400 subscribers. Thereafter it would sell at two guineas. In the event there were 303 subscribers named at the front of the book, of which some forty-nine were from the nobility or gentry, plus a handful of professional men, academics and booksellers. The rest were all tradespeople. So successful was the venture that a second edition appeared in 1755, almost identical to the first.

The St Martin's Lane premises comprised nos. 59, 60 and 61, on the right hand side of the street going north from Charing Cross (6) (no. 62 was eventually occupied by Thomas Chippendale Jnr in 1793). The firm's trade card described Chippendale and Rannie as 'Cabinet Makers and Upholsterers', indicating the wide range of services they provided. They could furnish and equip a whole house, from servants' rooms in the attics to family apartments and grand state rooms, including wallpapers, curtains, carpets, and kitchen equipment. Specialist work was probably out-sourced, including hardware and perhaps marquetry. The firm even provided an undertaking service. Chippendale himself probably no longer worked at the bench, but was fully occupied in design, liaising with clients and quality control. For important new commissions Chippendale would generally be recommended by the consultant architect, such as Robert Adam or John Carr. The architect would expect to be shown and approve Chippendale's proposals before they were executed.

Despite a serious workshop fire in April 1755, the furniture business thrived, and the first fully documented commissions (all Scottish) arrived in the late 1750s: from Lord Arniston (1757), the Duke of Atholl (1758) and — outstandingly — the Earl of Dumfries (1759). At the end of the decade, spurred on by a proposed new publication from his rivals, Ince and Mayhew, Chippendale prepared a third edition of the *Director* which eventually appeared in 1762. It contained 200 plates, 100 being entirely new, and included his vision of a fully mature Rococo style, while acknowledging the arrival of a new taste, the 'Antique' style which is now called neo-Classicism.

By the mid-1760s Chippendale's reputation was such that in November 1767 the *London Gazetteer and New Daily Advertiser* called him 'that celebrated artist, Mr. Chippendale, of St. Martin's Lane'. But earlier, in January 1766, James Rannie had died, plunging the business into financial crisis. Chippendale's money worries at this time are well documented, and it is probable that he never fully recovered from the financial damage caused by Rannie's debts. Stability only returned with a new partnership between Chippendale and the firm's former book-keeper, Thomas Haig, in 1770. It also included the shadowy figure of Henry Ferguson, an erstwhile colleague of James Rannie.

By the early 1770s Chippendale had mastered neo-Classicism as completely as he had the Rococo, and his furniture reached a peak of artistic and technical excellence in series of high profile commissions, of which Harewood House is the most famous. It is likely that during this time his son, Thomas Chippendale Jnr, began to take an increasingly active role in the business. Although firm evidence is lacking, major commissions of the late 1770s (for instance, the Great Drawing Room at Burton Constable Hall) show small but significant changes in design which seem to reveal Thomas Jnr's hand. By this

2 Thomas Bowles III after Antonio Canaletto, 1753, 'A View of Northumberland House, Charing Cross' etching. Northumberland Court was the alley leading from the arch immediately to the left of the great mansion. *British Museum*

time Chippendale himself was in his late fifties, and was probably glad to be transferring what must have been multiple and onerous responsibilities.

Chippendale's first wife, Catherine, died in August 1772. Apart from Thomas Jnr, almost nothing is known of their nine children (five boys and four girls). In August 1777 Chippendale married a second time, to Elizabeth Davis, who bore him three more children. It is likely that by this date he had largely retired from an active role in the firm, since he appears to have been living in Derry Street, Kensington (7). In early November 1779 Chippendale was in Hoxton, being treated for tuberculosis; he died there aged sixty-two, and was buried on 13 November 1779.

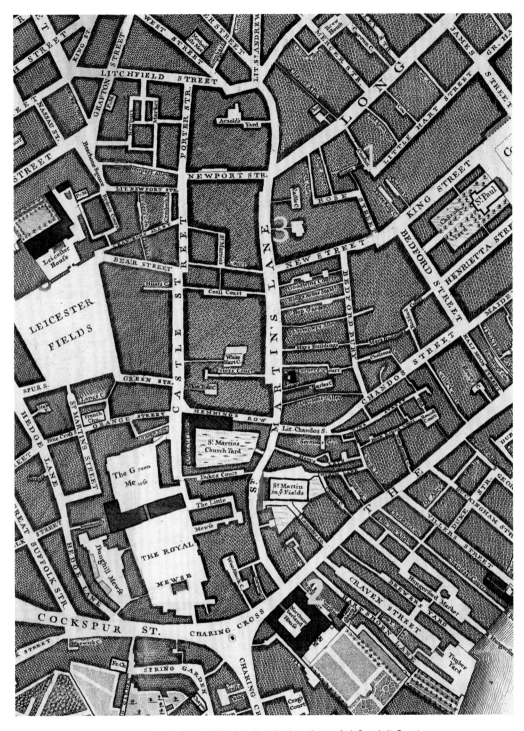

3 Detail from Rocque's map of London, 1746, showing the locations of: **1** Conduit Court,
2 Northumberland Court, **3** nos 59-61 St Martins Lane.

4 T. H. Shepherd, 'St Martin's Lane', 1846, watercolour. Chippendale's premises were on the left (east side) further towards the church of St. Martin's-in-the-Fields. *British Museum*.

THE

GENTLEMAN

AND

CABINET-MAKER's

DIRECTOR.

BEING A LARGE

COLLECTION

OF THE MOST

Elegant and Useful Designs of Houshold Furniture

IN THE

GOTHIC, CHINESE and MODERN TASTE:

Including a great VARIETY of

BOOK-CASES for LIBRARIES or Private ROOMS. COMMODES, LIBRARY and WRITING-TABLES, BUROES, BREAKFAST-TABLES, DRESSING and CHINA-TABLES, CHINA-CASES, HANGING-SHELVES,	TEA-CHESTS, TRAYS, FIRE-SCREENS, CHAIRS, SETTEES, SOPHA'S, BEDS, PRESSES and CLOATHS-CHESTS, PIER-GLASS SCONCES, SLAB FRAMES, BRACKETS, CANDLE-STANDS, CLOCK-CASES, FRETS,

AND OTHER

ORNAMENTS.

TO WHICH IS PREFIXED,

A Short EXPLANATION of the Five ORDERS of ARCHITECTURE,
and RULES of PERSPECTIVE;

WITH

Proper DIRECTIONS for executing the most difficult Pieces, the Mouldings being exhibited
at large, and the Dimensions of each DESIGN specified:

THE WHOLE COMPREHENDED IN

One Hundred and Sixty COPPER-PLATES, neatly Engraved,

Calculated to improve and refine the present TASTE, and suited to the Fancy and Circumstances of
Persons in all Degrees of Life.

Dulcique animos novitate tenebo. OVID.
Ludentis speciem dabit & torquebitur. HOR.

BY

THOMAS CHIPPENDALE,

Of St. *MARTIN's-LANE*, CABINET-MAKER.

LONDON,

Printed for the AUTHOR, and sold at his House in St. MARTIN's-LANE. MDCCLIV.
Also by T. OSBORNE, Bookseller, in Gray's-Inn; H. PIERS, Bookseller, in Holborn; R. SAYER, Print-
seller, in Fleetstreet; J. SWAN, near Northumberland-House, in the Strand. At EDINBURGH, by
Messrs. HAMILTON and BALFOUR: And at DUBLIN, by Mr. JOHN SMITH, on the Blind-Quay.

5 Thomas Chippendale, *The Gentleman and Cabinet-Maker's Director*, 1754, title page.
The Chippendale Society

KEY TO WORKSHOP PLAN

A Cabinet makers' shops, three storeys
B Shed with room above
C Open covered passage to yard, two storeys above
D Three storeys: ground floor, sheds and ware-rooms; first floor, glass room; upper floor with an open cockle (loft)
E Veneering room with feather room above
F Drying room with fireproof stone floor, with a German stove and oven; carpet room above
G Flue for German stove
H Store room and show-room
J Two storey building; ground floor, counting house, store room above
K Counting house
L Three storey building
M Upholsterers' shop and ware-room with German stove; wood seasoning stacks on roof

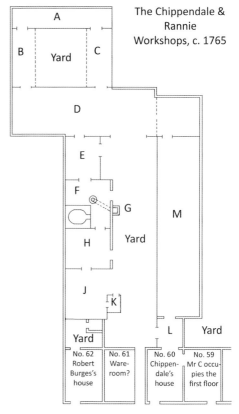

The Chippendale & Rannie Workshops, c. 1765

| A |
| B Yard C |
| D |
| E |
| F |
| G M |
| H Yard |
| J |
| K |
| L Yard |
| Yard |

| No. 62 Robert Burges's house | No. 61 Ware-room? | No. 60 Chippen-dale's house | No. 59 Mr C occu-pies the first floor |

St Martin's Lane

6 (right) Plan of the Chippendale and Rannie workshops, redrawn from the *Survey of London*.

7 (below) Derry Street, Kensington, *c.*1925. Chippendale's last years were spent in one of the terraced houses on the right.
Historic England

STYLE

The title page of the first edition of Chippendale's *Director* announced that it contained 'Designs of Household Furniture in the GOTHIC, CHINESE AND MODERN TASTE… calculated to improve and refine the present TASTE, and suited to the Fancy and Circumstances of Persons in all Degrees of Life'. It made clear that the author was presenting the three principle strands of contemporary design and suggesting how furniture made in these styles could be improved by well-trained craftsmen and also become known to a wider public. For an artisan without a metropolitan background or a long list of influential clients it was a bold and risky ambition.

'MODERN TASTE'

The 'Modern Taste' (also known at the time as 'French', 'Contrast' or the *genre pitturesque*) is the style today described as Rococo. It developed in France in the last years of Louis XIV as a reaction to the ponderous Classicism of the Baroque style. Its forms are essentially anti-Classical and derived from nature: C and S scrolls, trailing and exuberant leaf forms, watery and aquatic decoration, and above all the serpentine line which, as its great advocate William Hogarth wrote, 'leads the eye a wanton chase' (1).

Chippendale may first have encountered the 'Modern Taste' while still in Yorkshire if he had become involved in the prevailing craze for re-building and furnishing numerous country houses. Once in London, however, he naturally gravitated to St. Martin's Lane and the centre of the new movement. His affinity with the style can be seen in his preparatory drawings for the *Director*, particularly those prefaced by the word 'French' (2), and are the epitome of the style as understood in England. His natural affinity with carving — for which the Rococo style is so suited — can be seen in the brilliantly naturalistic figure of a crane which once surmounted a day bed at Harewood (3), and also in the numerous designs for pier glasses and other mirrors (4).

Who taught Chippendale to draw with such fluency and confidence? One contender might be his future collaborator, Matthias Darly, a versatile and prolific draughtsman and engraver who also advertised himself as a drawing master. Another might be Matthias Lock, a brilliant draughtsman and carver whose drawings were also engraved and published and who taught the virtuoso carver Thomas Johnson.

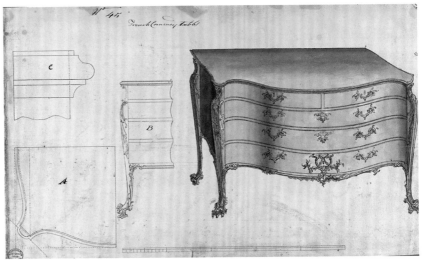

1 (top) Thomas Chippendale, *Invitation card*, 1753, engraved by Matthias Darly.
The Chippendale Society

2 (bottom) Thomas Chippendale, Drawing for a French commode table, 1753.
Metropolitan Museum of Art, Rogers Fund 1920 20.40.2 (57)

3 Figure of a crane, 1769, from a
domed couch bed at Harewood House.
The Chippendale Society

4 Pier glass, *c.*1762–65, attributed to the Chippendale workshop. *Private Collection*

The acclaim with which the *Director* was met emboldened Chippendale into providing even more ambitious designs for the third edition of 1762. For the Modern style he devised new towering canopied beds, festooned toilet tables (5) pier glasses, tables and French commodes, sometimes in an almost uncontrolled fantasy. Nevertheless, he continued to deny his critics who, perhaps understandably, saw the designs 'as so many specious drawings, impossible to be worked off', saying that he was 'confident I can convince all Noblemen, Gentlemen, or others… that every design in the book can be improved, both as to beauty and enrichment, in the execution of it'… by himself. Ironically, Chippendale's documented work from this period is rare, but is represented supremely in the Dumfries House commission (6).

CHINESE CHIPPENDALE

By the time the *Director* appeared in 1754 the popularity of the Chinese style (sometimes confusingly known as 'Indian') had almost reached fever pitch. It had developed as a fanciful vision of the Orient, largely taken from imagery found on porcelain, textiles and lacquer and featured fantastical landscapes, with dragons, ho-ho birds, pagodas and fretted balustrades, populated with Chinese figures. A newspaper reported somewhat critically: 'According to the present whim everything is Chinese or in the Chinese taste; or as it is more modestly expressed, *partly after the Chinese manner*. Chairs, tables, chimneypieces and frames for looking glasses… are all reduced to this new-fangled standard'. A number of contemporary publications, including Darly and Edwards', *A New Book of Chinese Designs* (1754) had also encapsulated its new and essentially Rococo character of whimsicality and playfulness.

In essence the style was another reaction to the Palladian mainstream, easily co-existing with the equally popular Modern and Gothic styles, each one

5 Thomas Chippendale, *Drawing for a lady's dressing table*, 1761. Metropolitan Museum of Art, Rogers Fund 1920 20.40.2 (65)

6 Armchair, 1759. One of a suite delivered to the Earl of Dumfries. *The Great Steward of Scotland's Dumfries House Trust. Photo Christie's Images*

7 Lady's dressing table, *c.* 1760. Attributed to the Chippendale workshop and probably made for Lady Arniston of Arniston House, Midlothian. *National Museums on Merseyside (Lady Lever Art Gallery).*

8 'India Picture' made from a collage of hand-painted Chinese wallpaper, *c*.1770–71. Supplied for the Yellow Chintz Bedroom at Harewood House. *The Chippendale Society*

9 Chair, *c*.1755–70. The design is taken from Plate XXVIII of the 1762 *Director*. Probably made by a regional furniture maker. *National Museums on Merseyside (Lady Lever Art Gallery). [Photo Clare Bates]*

10 (above) Japanned commode table, *c.*1771. Supplied for the Alcove Bed Chamber at Nostell Priory. *The National Trust, Nostell Priory*

11 (left) Secretaire, 1773, veneered in Chinese lacquer. Made for the State Bedroom at Harewood House. *Leeds Museums and Galleries, Temple Newsam House*

feeding off the others' impulses. Therefore it is never possible to be dogmatic about style when attempting to categorise Chippendale's executed work: frequently he inserts a deliberate solecism or an ambiguous motif which defies explanation yet which contributes to an entirely satisfactory effect. As the anonymous writer in *The World* wrote in 1754, 'how much of late we are improved in architecture not merely by the adoption of what we call Chinese, nor by the restoration of what we call Gothic, but by the happy mixture of both'. The result, like Lady Arniston's dressing table (7) is a fortuitous amalgam: its serpentine shape is topped by a pagoda-like canopy, while the carved astragals of the side cupboards combine suggestions of both Gothic and Chinese frets.

The 1754 *Director* contained sixty-four plates with furniture of a Chinese character, over one-third of the total. Like the Modern style it was particularly suitable for carving. There were pier glasses with birds and dragons, beds and sophas with pagoda or trellised canopies, china cases with upturned eaves and bells, bookshelves and china shelves with fretwork sides and brackets. Many of the items were associated with interiors belonging to women: bedrooms, dressing rooms and drawing rooms, for some of which Chippendale could oblige with appropriate hangings of 'India paper' (8).

Some critics deplored the Chinese style for its lack of discipline, since there appeared to be no generally accepted rules or guidelines, let alone any acknowledgment of precedents to be found in real Oriental furniture. Chippendale was evidently aware of this and was determined to reform its worst excesses while at the same time make the style more appropriate for everyday living. He provided designs for nine chairs 'in the present Chinese manner' which he hoped would 'improve that taste... it having yet never arrived to any perfection; doubtless it might be lost without seeing its beauty: as it admits of the greatest variety, I think it the most useful of any other'. They were clearly experimental for 'there has been none like them yet made' (9).

'Japanning', or painted decoration in the Chinese style, was once again as popular as it had been in the late seventeenth century (10). It was an expensive luxury, while real Oriental lacquer, provided by the clients themselves ('your own Japann'), could be made up by Chippendale into smart new French-inspired pieces (11). However, the 1762 *Director* saw a marked decline in the number of Chinese pieces, perhaps because in form (but not decoration), the style was not compatible with the new wave of Classicism which was just then coming into fashion.

GOTHIC

Gothic (or 'Gothick') was already well established as a popular, often whimsical, style for small buildings and interiors by the time the *Director* was

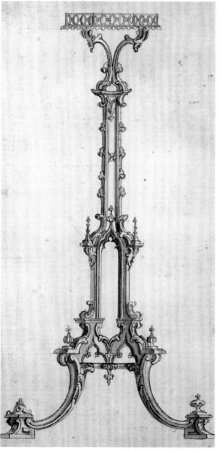

12 (above) Writing Table, *c.* 1760.
Attributed to the Chippendale workshop.
York Civic Trust, Fairfax House.

13 (left) Thomas Chippendale, *Drawing
for a candlestand*, 1760. *The
Chippendale Society*

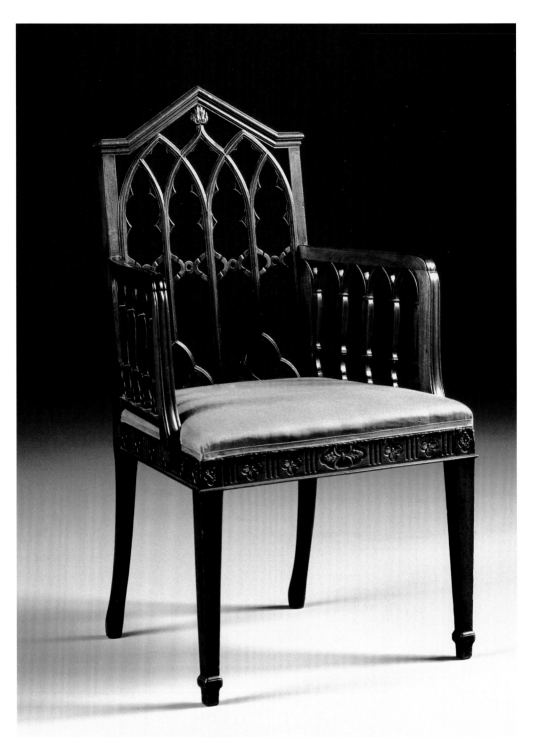

14 Armchair, adapted from Plate XVII of the 1762 *Director*. Probably made by Gillow's for Muncaster Castle, 1784. *Birmingham Museums Trust, Soho House*

published in 1754. It was popularly associated with the historical glories of the Medieval past but there was little understanding of the style's evolution, structure, or the coherence of its ornamental vocabulary. Its most obvious decorative features — delicate frets, cusped friezes, pointed tracery, ogee arches, crocketed pinnacles, clustered columns and finials — were seen as a quarry for embellishing otherwise conventional structures. This attitude began to change under the influence of the romantic antiquarians, of whom Horace Walpole was the most famous.

There were few known Medieval precedents for Gothic furniture and, until the publication of the *Director*, only a handful of experiments had been attempted to adapt the style to modern and practical needs. Batty Langley's *Gothic Architecture Improved* (1742) and subsequent publications had tried to impose the language of Classicism and the Orders for 'architectural' furnishings. Chippendale took full cognizance of this in his designs for certain types of furniture such as bookcases or library tables on which Gothic decorative motifs were overlaid on a Classical structure (**12**).

Chippendale clearly enjoyed designing in Gothic, intending to bring the style to a new and wider audience, and he described how certain designs could 'be of use to those that are unacquainted with this sort of work'. His real achievement was to show how it could be used legitimately in the design of everyday objects, irrespective of structural purpose or 'correctness'. The effect of its decorative richness can be seen most fully in a drawing for a candlestand (**13**). He was scathing about those who considered his designs, 'especially those after the Gothick and Chinese Manner', to be too fanciful or difficult. They were widely imitated: Gillows of Lancaster copied a set of arcaded chairs from Plate XVII (1762) for Lord Muncaster in 1784 (**14**). In all, Chippendale provided twenty four plates for Gothic furniture in the 1754 *Director* and twenty three in 1762. They ranged from furniture for 'Halls, Passages or Summer-Houses', to libraries, dining rooms and bedrooms.

CHIPPENDALE AND THE 'ANTIQUE'

Chippendale acknowledged the supreme importance of an understanding of the rules of Classical architecture for cabinet makers in the first ringing sentence of the 1754 *Director*: 'Of all the ARTS which are either improved or ornamented by Architecture, that of CABINET MAKING is not only the most useful and ornamental, but capable of receiving as great assistance from it as any whatever'. This was followed up by plates of the five Orders plagiarised directly from James Gibbs's *The Rules for Drawing the Several Parts of Architecture* (1732).

Many of the illustrations in the 1754 edition show furniture based on Classical forms: temple-fronted and pedimented bookcases, trabeated tables, pilastered clock cases, and library and dressing tables as implied triumphal 'arches'. Chippendale's purpose, as he saw it, was to show how these Classical forms could be legitimately overlaid by ornament taken from profoundly anti-Classical sources: Gothic, Chinese and Modern. But change was in the air in the late 1750s and early 60s, and anticipating this Chippendale began a series of new designs which were ultimately incorporated into a new and third edition of the *Director* in 1762. Perhaps surprisingly, about a dozen reflected advanced thinking from France, where the new Classical revival, the *gout grec* was under way. Their architects and designers were highly cerebral in their approach, but at first this was entirely lacking in Chippendale's interpretation, where the new forms and ornamental details were treated as decorative accessories. This attitude changed profoundly when he began to collaborate with Robert Adam, the Scottish architect whose name is forever associated with early neo-Classicism (or the 'Antique', as the new style was usually known).

In 1758 Adam had returned from Italy with portfolios of drawings from Classical sources and a determination to revolutionise taste and design in Britain. His interpretation of the 'true style of [ancient Classical] decoration' was based on 'the rise and fall, the advance and recess and other diversity of forms' and the 'variety of light mouldings' he had encountered in the ancient sites of Rome and Spalatro. His use of 'invention' — a term much used at this time to describe the adaptation of generic ideas and motifs — was demonstrated to great effect in his *Works in Architecture* (1773).

Although Adam's interiors were brilliant essays in invention he could rely on almost no precedents for furniture design nor did he have any knowledge of how the new style could be applied to free-standing three dimensional models. After some experiments, both Adam and Chippendale were able to provide solutions acceptable to their clients. The magnificent armchair, part of a suite made for Sir Laurence Dundas in 1765, is the only example of Chippendale's furniture for which a bespoke drawing by Adam exists (**15**). It retains a basically Rococo serpentine form but is overlaid with an abundance of Classical ornament in low relief. The plethora of decoration suggests that both architect and craftsman were demonstrating all the possibilities of the new style but were still unsure as to its practical application. The same could be said for the Library Armchair for Nostell Priory of 1767 (**16**) which is a similar self-consciously Antique form over-charged with Classical ornament yet still retaining vestiges of the Rococo.

A Mature Style

After a hesitant start Adam and Chippendale soon came to understand how the simpler forms and repetitive motifs of the Antique style could be used coherently and were capable of great variety. The lyre-back chair — symbol of Apollo and first used by Chippendale at Nostell — was produced with variations and refinements for a number of different clients (**17**). Motifs such as

15 Armchair, 1765. Part of a suite of armchairs and sofas made for Sir Lawrence Dundas, designed by Robert Adam and made by the Chippendale workshop. *Victoria and Albert Museum*

16 Armchair, 1767. From a suite made for the new library at Nostell Priory, Yorkshire. *The National Trust, Nostell Priory*

17 Armchair, *c.* 1773. From a suite made for the new library at Brocket Hall,
Hertfordshire. *The Chippendale Society*

sunken paterae or Greek keys were used on a wide variety of different furniture and became something of a signature.

Although the process has gone almost unrecorded it seems clear that Adam developed a close professional relationship with Chippendale. The architect required his interiors to be harmoniously furnished, to link visually and aesthetically with their architectural features without being pedantic or dull. Chippendale could supply this effortlessly with an instinctive grasp of form and ornament and their proper uses. Marquetry decoration was the ideal medium in which demonstrate the new repertory of ornament (as carving had been for Rococo), together with judicious use of gilt brass mounts (18 & 19).

Chippendale clearly understood Adam's decorative repertoire and it is telling that at Harewood — probably the biggest commission for both parties — there are no drawings by Adam for furniture. When he first arrived there in July 1767 Chippendale wrote that he needed to make 'Many designs & knowing that I had time Enough I went to York to do them'. He was as confident working in the new style as he had been in the old ones.

Chippendale's relationship with other architects working in the Antique style could be less harmonious. Sir William Chambers considered himself 'a very pretty connoisseur of furniture' and even dared to suggest that Chippendale's designs for furniture at Melbourne House 'may be improved a little'. Some of these pieces might, indeed, have something of Chambers' hand in them (20).

Throughout this period the influence of France remained strong. Despite the temporary interruption of the Seven Years War, Paris was the destination of everyone — craftsmen or consumers — who aspired to be truly fashionable. Chippendale was certainly there in 1768 and the following year was caught attempting to import five dozen French chair frames as 'lumber', thus avoiding high import duties. In addition, leading French *ébenistes* and *menuisiers* were known to visit London and it is inconceivable they would not make contact with Chippendale and other makers as potential business partners. A whole group of oval and shaped back chairs, armchairs, and bergères, are often difficult to distinguish from their French counterparts (21).

By the mid-1770s the Antique style in interiors was becoming increasingly refined, and by this stage Thomas Chippendale Jnr was without doubt taking increasing responsibility for the artistic side of the business, so that it is often difficult to determine where the father's work ended and the son's began. Chippendale Jnr was to make his mark as an independent designer with the publication of his own *Sketches of Ornament* (1779).

18 (above) Detail of a Pier table, 1775. Made for the Yellow Damask Sitting Room at Harewood House, Yorkshire. *Private Collection*

19 (left) Cellaret, *c.*1771. Made for the Dining Room at Harewood as part of a sideboard ensemble. *The Harewood House Trust*

20 Cabinet, one of a pair, *c.* 1773. Made for Melbourne House, Piccadilly, London.
Trustees of the Firle Estate Settlement [Photo Edward Reeves]

21 Armchair, *c.*1774. Made for the Tapestry Drawing Room at Newby Hall, Yorkshire. The suite is the only furniture made by the Chippendale workshop which retains its original upholstery. *Mr and Mrs Richard Compton*

CUSTOMERS

WHY CHOOSE CHIPPENDALE?

Chippendale's customers included theatre managers, merchants, politicians, country baronets and peers of the realm. The common factor was not age, geography, political allegiance or social status, but money. Chippendale's workshop was one of perhaps a dozen in London catering to an elite clientele who demanded the best furnishings that money could buy. Some customers, such Sir Lawrence Dundas, hedged their bets and patronised several different workshops, perhaps believing that competition got them more choice or a better price (1). Others, like Edwin Lascelles, seem to have used Chippendale exclusively.

Why chose Chippendale and not one of his competitors? The nexus of big Yorkshire commissions might suggest regional solidarity played a role in supporting the Otley-born tradesman, but on its own this would have mattered little to the hard-headed Lascelles or the sophisticated and well-travelled William Weddell. Robert's Adams's recommendation must also have counted for much, but Adam would not have risked his reputation and his livelihood purely out of personal liking. Chippendale clearly had something special, and rich people were prepared to pay for it. His furniture, while reflecting stylistic trends of the day, was always original and distinctive while remaining practical in use. While many craftsmen could make sound furniture, and many artists could dream up beautiful designs, Chippendale could do both. He combined solid craftsmanship with artistic flair in a way that few competitors could match.

FURNITURE FROM STOCK

Even the wealthiest households needed ordinary furniture for everyday use and for immediate purchase, and so it was usual for furniture makers to keep a range of stock to suit. Pattern chairs and parts of chairs, small tables and parts of tables, dressing chests and dressing glasses were available from stock or could quickly be assembled from ready-made components (2). Many of these items were so mundane and generic that they differed only slightly from furniture supplied by other furniture makers (3), and sometimes the making of such pieces was outsourced to local makers, as happened at Harewood House (4). But even if from stock, Chippendale's furniture was always bespoke to some

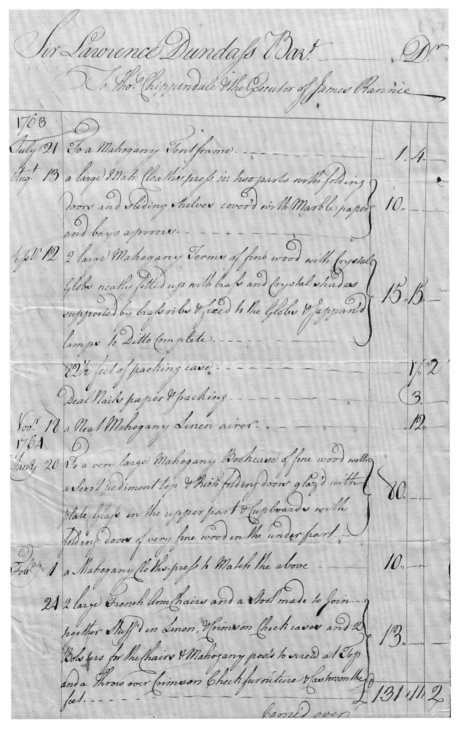

1 Bill for furniture supplied to Sir Lawrence Dundas, 1763. *North Yorkshire County Record Office*

2 Hexagon table, *c.*1770, attributed to the
Chippendale workshop. *Leeds Museums
and Galleries, Temple Newsam House*

degree. Every piece emerging from his workshop was different for each customer, even if only in size or small details. Chippendale's hand can usually be discerned not only in the generic models he invented but also his 'signature' motifs: key frets, or paterae and swags in certain combinations, distinctive details of arm or foot design, and so on. Many of these continued into the years when Chippendale Jnr had taken over managing the workshops.

Bespoke commissions

The big money was made in bespoke commissions and these, moreover, allowed Chippendale to demonstrate the full range of his talents as a designer and furniture maker. In some cases, such as the fitting out of Sir William Constable's London apartment in 1774, Chippendale probably dealt directly with the client, discussing room colours, types of fabric, levels of trim, the quantity and type of seating, number of case pieces &c. These largely cosmetic alterations to an existing house did not require the services of an architect, but for more ambitious projects, which involved building and furnishing a new house or remodelling an existing one, it was often the architect who stood between the client and the furniture maker. Thus good relations between Chippendale and the architect were as important to the success of a commission as between Chippendale and the client. Fortunately, Chippendale seems to have got on well with both James Paine and Robert Adam, and these men were probably vital in securing major commissions such as at Brocket Hall (James Paine), and at Newby Hall and Harewood House (Robert Adam). At Melbourne House, on the other hand, the relationship between Chippendale and the architect Sir William Chambers was not good. Where trust and goodwill existed between all parties Chippendale had a great deal of latitude in his work, and the key to success was the degree to which he could realise his client's vision within the agreed budget.

The work fell into several clearly defined stages. First, the initial agreement on what was required — how many rooms were to be furnished, and what they should contain. Lists of furniture which reflect these discussions survive for Nostell Priory and Aske Hall. Second, the production of initial designs, agreement on final designs and agreement of estimates. Third, the execution of the designs by the Chippendale workshops, and finally the delivery and installation.

Because creating new and original designs was expensive, Chippendale developed several ranges of furniture which relied on a common basic model which could be modified in detail to make each commission unique. His various models of lyre-back and oval-back chairs are prime examples of this practise (5).

Other services

Chippendale's firm did not just make furniture. On major commissions workmen were sent to measure up, make plans and estimates, consult and liaise with other tradesmen. Once the job was underway, they unpacked and set up the furniture, mended any damage which had occurred in transit and made *in situ* alterations where necessary. They hung pier glasses, put up curtains, applied silk wall coverings or printed wallpaper (6), and fitted wall trims (7). On occasions, as at Harewood and Paxton, Chippendale even designed wallpaper and had it made to order. For David Garrick and Sir William Robinson Chippendale arranged removals and storage, and he was frequently asked to repair furniture. Some of the repair work was very mundane indeed — 'Repairing a rush bottomed chair 1/6d', or 'A new handle to a Silver Coffee Pot'. This sort of work was scarcely worth the trouble, but customers expected it. Chippendale would even arrange for beds to be aired and mattresses turned and, like many of his rivals, he could either rent out or lend furniture for short term use. He kept a stock of Oriental and European carpets, and could have carpets woven at Axminster to customers' specifications. He also kept stocks of china and glassware, mostly used to fit out dressing tables, washstands and night tables.

Most upholsterers could arrange funerals. In 1772 Chippendale charged £121 15s 11d for arranging the funeral of Lady Heathcote (8). His charges included the coffins (lead-lined inner and velvet-covered outer) and their brassware, hiring the pallbearers, supplying accessories for the dozens of mourners — hatbands, gloves scarves and hoods — hiring and fitting out the hearse (complete with ostrich-plumed horses), and taking care of all expenses and arrangements for the cortege between London and the family seat at Normanton Park, Rutland. Chippendale's was a truly comprehensive, cradle-to-grave furnishing concern.

Awkward customers

No tradesman, no matter how successful and celebrated, could afford to offend a powerful client, particularly when that client's patronage extended to his wider family, friends, political and business associates. When bills needed to be paid it was difficult for tradesmen like Chippendale to put pressure on their clients, and many were slow payers. When they did pay, it tended to be in bills of exchange or promissory notes, often dated weeks or months ahead, rather than cash. To be fair, it was often equally difficult for the clients; they had multiple demands on their money, with large households to run (usually more than one), family, servants and staff to pay for, and they often received their income only quarterly or even yearly. As Sir Edward Knatchbull put it: '… as I receive my rents once a year so I pay my Tradesmens' Bills once a year'. The

3 Tray, supplied to the Earl of Dumfries, 1763. *The Great Steward of Scotland's Dumfries House Trust. Photo Christie's images*

shortage of ready money also explains the long duration of many commissions, for they could only progress at the rate at which the client was able to pay for them.

The most difficult situation for a tradesman was when he himself was under financial pressure at the same time as his clients were slow to pay. It is no accident that one of Chippendale's most contentious professional relationships, with Sir Rowland Winn of Nostell Priory, occurred at the time in the late 1760s when he was beset by creditors after James Rannie's death (**9**)). But Sir Rowland was disposed to be difficult from the start, for his complaints began even before Chippendale sent in his bills. He complained that work was not completed on time and threatened to damage Chippendale's business: '… You May Expect to find me as great an Enemy as I ever was Your Friend… [I] shall take care to Acquaint those Gentlemen that I have Recommended you to & desire that they will oblige me in employing some other person …'. In the face of such threats Chippendale had no option but to be complaisant. Sir Rowland's complaints may have had some foundation, but they also enabled him to establish a position of social and moral superiority which he exploited to his advantage.

In the case of Sir Edward Knatchbull, of Mersham le Hatch in Kent, Chippendale seems to have done his best to satisfy a tetchy and demanding customer who was continually worried about money. The fact that Knatchbull continued to employ Chippendale over a period of at least ten years suggests that, on the whole, the work was satisfactory and the bills perfectly reasonable. Perhaps Chippendale just added on a percentage, secure in the knowledge that Knatchbull would routinely require him to reduce the bill by the same amount. It would be wrong to assume that tradesmen were entirely powerless when dealing with awkward customers.

4 (above) Working drawing for a tea table, *c*.1773, supplied by Thomas Chippendale to Christopher Theakston, a local carver at Harewood. *The Harewood House Trust*

5 (facing page, top) Drawing for a chair, *c*.1778, showing alternative treatments for legs, arms and backs. Inscribed 'Chipindale'. *The Burton Constable Foundation*

6 (facing page, bottom) Wallpaper fragment, 1760, from 26 Soho Square, London, probably supplied by the Chippendale workshop to Sir William Robinson. *Historic England*

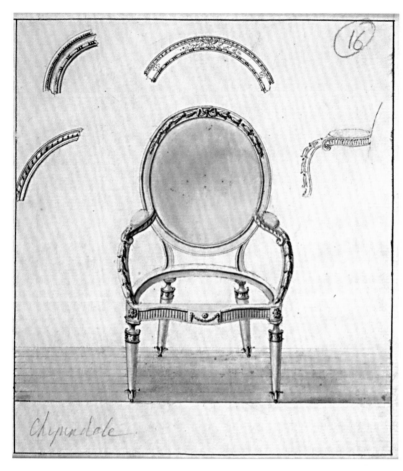

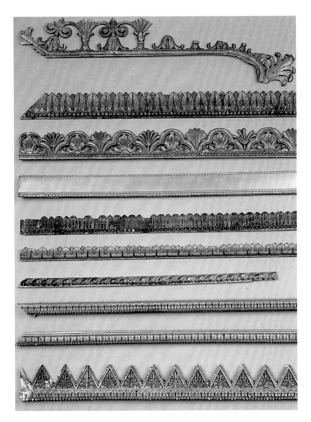

7 (left) Wall borders, *c.*1770–75, made for various rooms at Harewood House. *The Chippendale Society*

8 (below) Coffin furniture, 1772, supplied by the Chippendale workshop for the coffin of Lady Heathcote. *The Chippendale Society*

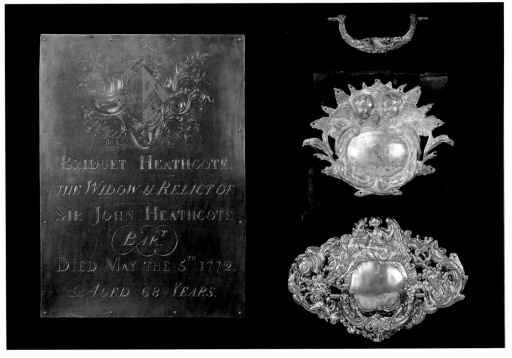

S[r] Rowland   London Sep[r] 27 [th] 1769
                    answerd this Lett Oct[r] y[e] 16th 1769

I hope that you will be so good as
to Excuse the liberty I have taken in
in Writing to you, but it is to infor
me you that y[e] Note which you was.
so kind as to give me has ben due five
or six days and it has been presented
for payment Several times it lay
at S[r] George Colebrooks, S[r] George
was so kind as to give me Cash for it.
and he has sent to me to insist of
the payment which is absolutely
out of My power at present to do
if you Can by any Means Send y[e]
Mony to town it will save My
Cridet other wifes I shall be ruened,
your things are all finished and the
will be sent away by y[e] very first
Waggon — I am your very Hum[le] Ser[t]
                    Tho[s] Chippendale

9 Letter from Thomas Chippendale to Sir Rowland Winn, 27 September 1769.
The Chippendale Society

LEGACY

A large proportion of subscribers to the *Director* was based outside London, with both Scotland and Yorkshire being strongly represented. This bias almost certainly arose from personal connections, with Yorkshire through Chippendale's family and early training in York, and in Scotland through his Scottish business partner, James Rannie. There were other subscribers in Lancaster, Liverpool, Nottingham and some smaller provincial towns.

This wide geographical distribution accounts for the quantity of provincial furniture based on *Director* designs which survives today. Some of it is high quality, the product of sophisticated urban workshops, but much is more obviously provincial, and often made from native rather than imported woods (1). Many provincial furniture makers probably never saw an original version of the *Director* but made copies from furniture seen in rival workshops or in customers' homes. As well as making furniture after *Director* patterns, some provincial makers 'borrowed' Chippendale's designs to use in their own advertising (2).

Recognising the importance of European markets, Chippendale produced a French version of the *Director* in 1762 – *Guide Du Tapissier, De L'Ebeniste*. There is little evidence it had much impact in France itself, but that was not the point: French was the international language of diplomacy, literature and culture. Copies were acquired by, among others, Catherine the Great of Russia and a number of German noblemen. In much of Europe there was already a well-established market for British furniture, particularly in Germany, Scandinavia, Spain, Portugal and Russia. Furniture derived from British models can be found in all these places, and while few can be related directly to Chippendale designs, they are broadly indicative of the appeal of British Rococo.

Copies of the *Director* may have reached the British North American colonies as early as 1755. A number of prominent 18th-century American furniture-makers are known to have owned copies and some even used Chippendale's designs for their own trade cards. However, the highly decorated Rococo style did not find universal favour among the generally pragmatic colonists, and the book appears to have had a major impact in only two furniture-making centres, Philadelphia and Charleston (3).

1 Chair, c. 1765. *York Civic Trust, Fairfax House*

2 Trade card of Robert Barker, York, 1762. *Simon Redburn*

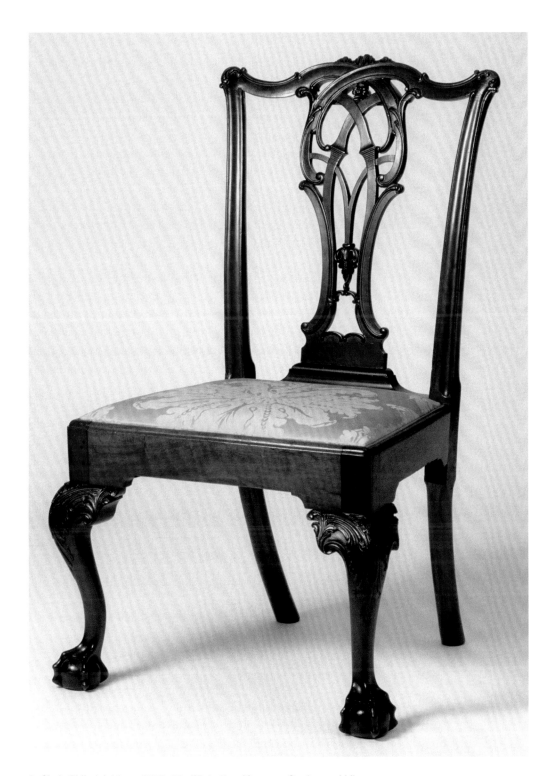

3 Chair, Philadelphia, *c.*1763–80. *Winterthur Museum, Garden and Library*

THE NINETEENTH-CENTURY CHIPPENDALE REVIVAL

By the end of the eighteenth century the style that made Chippendale famous – the Rococo – was out of date, quaint and old fashioned. But among some designers and furniture-makers Chippendale's significance was still acknowledged, and his reputation was enhanced by the publication, about 1834, of *A Collection of Ornamental Designs ... chiefly after Thomas Chippendale* by the publisher John Weale (4). Ironically, this re-issue of eighteenth-century engravings contained nothing by Chippendale himself, but it did re-awaken interest in the British Rococo and the work of Thomas Chippendale. By the 1850s the phrase 'Chippendale style' was commonly used to describe all British Rococo furniture. Official recognition of Chippendale's status came in 1905, with the installation of a large full-length statue on the façade of the Victoria and Albert Museum.

In the decade immediately prior to the First World War (1914–18) the 'Chippendale' style was widely popular in Britain, especially among those with conservative tastes. It offered a safe alternative to the radical ideas of British Arts & Crafts and European Art Nouveau, while at the same time allowing a harmless flirtation with exotic themes such as Chinoiserie and Rococo (5). In an increasingly dangerous and volatile world, the 'Chippendale style' embodied quality, craftsmanship and traditional British values (6).

In the United States, the Colonial Revival movement of the late 19th and early twentieth centuries spawned its own Chippendale Revival, and 'Chippendale' is now a generally accepted term for some forms of eighteenth century American furniture. The design used for the 2004 US Mail 'American Design' series stamp is based on a Philadelphia chair of the 1760s (7).

CHIPPENDALE IN TWENTIETH-CENTURY POPULAR CULTURE

At the beginning of the twentieth century the name Chippendale was firmly associated both with high quality furniture-making and with a certain old-fashioned British style, epitomised by the whimsical parlour song, *Chintz and Chippendale* written by Daisy McGeoch, a well-known American composer of popular ballads (8).

In the second half of the century, the name Chippendale was adopted for a variety of unlikely commercial products because it had guaranteed brand recognition. 'Chip and Dale' were two chipmunk cartoon characters created by the Walt Disney cartoon studios in 1943. The comedy double act initially featured alongside established Disney characters such as Donald Duck, but in the 1950s they starred in three full-length cartoons. A number of Chip and Dale comic books were also published between 1955 and 1984. In 1989 Chip and Dale were revived for a new series, *Chip 'n Dale Rescue Rangers*, which has spawned spin-offs for TV and video games which are still available today. In 2014 Walt Disney Pictures announced a live action movie combined with CGI.

4 (top) John Weale, *Ornamental Designs ... after Thomas Chippendale*, frontispiece, *c.* 1834. *The Chippendale Society*

5 (bottom) Richard Jack, *The Chinese Chippendale Drawing Room*, Buckingham Palace, 1926. *Royal Collection Trust / © Her Majesty Queen Elizabeth II*

DESIGN FOR LIBRARY IN THE CHIPPENDALE STYLE.

6 (top) Gillows of Lancaster and London, *Design for a Library in the Chippendale Style*, *c.*1910. *Leeds Museums and Galleries, Temple Newsam House*

7 (bottom) Sheet of US mail postage stamps, American Design series, 2004. *The Chippendale Society*

© 2003 USPS

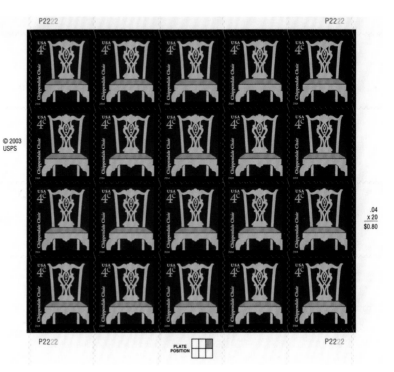

The Chippendales are an all-male dance troupe created in 1979 by the owners of the Destiny II nightclub in Los Angeles. They were named after the club's Chippendale-style furniture; the aim was to solve the club's financial difficulties by attracting a new, up-market and all female audience. The Chippendales' combination of slick choreography and male striptease was an instant success, and the troupe now performs in a purpose-built theatre in Las Vegas, as well as on tour, and has a worldwide following.

The British film comedy *The Full Monty* (1997), about a group of unemployed Yorkshire miners raising money with a striptease act, was inspired by *The Chippendales*.

CHIPPENDALE TODAY AND TOMORROW

The Chippendale name is still powerfully associated with quality, craftsmanship and tradition, but it is interpreted in many different ways. Venturi/Scott Brown's *Chippendale Chair with Grandmother pattern* (1983–84) is an amusing and subversive caricature of traditional taste, combining a Chippendale-type chair shape with a 1983 fabric design called 'Grandmother pattern'. It is made from moulded plywood, but nevertheless proved too expensive (and perhaps too idiosyncratic) for popular appeal (**9**).

Traditional furniture still has wide appeal, and faithful reproductions of Chippendale furniture are made all over the world. One of the biggest markets is in Asia, where abundant raw materials and low labour costs allow reproduction Chippendale chairs to be made for less than £50. In the United Kingdom a number of manufacturers pride themselves on matching the quality and workmanship of the eighteenth-century originals, and their furniture commands very high prices, both new and second hand (**10**). For some buyers this combines the best of both worlds — the style and quality of the eighteenth century with the robustness and reliability of the twenty-first. At a more mundane level, there are kitchen manufacturers, joiners, builders, decorators and other trades in the UK which use the name Chippendale to sell their services and products. For example, Chippendale Kitchens is a Yorkshire-based kitchen design and manufacturing company whose marketing slogan is 'Unmistakably British'. While Thomas Chippendale never had to design kitchens for a living, he would undoubtedly have endorsed the qualities of quality, craftsmanship and innovation which are still associated with his name.

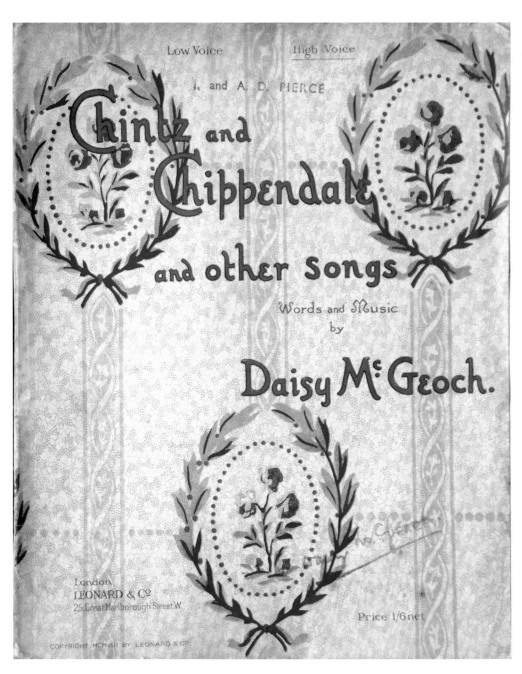

8 Music score for *Chintz and Chippendal*e, by Daisy McGeoch, 1918. *The Chippendale Society*

9 Robert Venturi and Denise Scott Brown, *Chippendale Chair with Grandmother Pattern*,
1983–84. *Courtesy Venturi Scott Brown and Associates, Inc/V&A Museum*

10   Bookcase model 5000, made by Arthur Brett & Sons Ltd, *c.* 2000.
Arthur Brett & Sons, Ltd